THE POSITION AND COURSE OF THE SOUTH.

THE

POSITION AND COURSE

OF

THE SOUTH.

BY WM. H. TRESCOT, ESQ.

CHARLESTON:
STEAM POWER-PRESS OF WALKER & JAMES.
1850.

PREFACE.

This pamphlet has been prepared and published at the request of those whose years, position and reputation, entitled their suggestions to respectful attention. If it meets their views, and aids in the slightest degree to strengthen Southern resolution, the author will feel grateful for the opportunity afforded him to perform even so small a service. The views it attempts to illustrate are not new, but they are Southern, and the fact, that in widely separated portions of our Southern country these opinions have impressed themselves upon minds different in temper, proves that we are beginning to think for ourselves—the first step towards acting for ourselves.

WM. HENRY TRESCOT.

October 12*th*, 1850.

THE POSITION AND COURSE OF THE SOUTH.

If history teaches any one lesson more emphatically than another, it is, that political institutions are never destroyed by influences foreign to themselves. Wherever, therefore in the history of government, there have been two contending classes, the success of the one has been achieved by the inconsistency of the other. The reformation was begun by a Catholic Priest. The feudal system was destroyed by absolute monarchs. The revolution of 1688 was the work of the whig aristocracy, as was the reform bill of a later period—and the French revolution, so often misquoted, was the joint labour of infidel Priests and democrat nobles.

And the warning which points this universal lesson, assumes a special significance at times like the present, when the marked characteristic of political life is the violent and uncompromising antagonism of great interests. Look to what quarter you may of the civilized world, and every where, government which should be almost judicial in its decision upon the complicated claims of national interests, has become simply the executive expression of a triumpant class. And every where great and contending interests struggle for power, not as a trust, but as a monopoly. In governments, the most consolidated—amid populations the most homogeneous, this truth is illustrating itself with destructive energy. What, for example, is now the great political difficulty in England, but that there two classes, two great interests are contending for legislative power—the landholder and the manufacturer. The one reasons thus: The feudal system carved England into great estates—to the crown—to the church—to the nobles each its share. The fundamental relation from the king to the crown, was that of landlord and tenant—of owner and occupier. The revenues of the crown came from land and the landholders represented the productive power of the nation. From this system proceeded the whole past history of England. Thence sprung that magnificent Common Law, broad and sure in its foundations as the soil, and as varied and prolific in its rich results—thence rose that life of exquisite civilization, the product of past energy and present cultivation, and thence only can come the power to preserve whence came the vigour to create. If England is to be the free monarchy of its past history, it must be the England of landholders. And the logical consequences are limited representation, and the corn laws. The other reasons thus: England has falsified the conditions of feudal life—the basis of her empire is no longer English soil—her colonial territories represent no connection of landlord and tenant—the crown no longer draws its revenue from royal forests—the sails of Liverpool, and the looms of Manchester, symbolize the relation of capital and labour. From this new relation must England's future history flow; thence must spring the controlling power of foreign markets; the mighty trade of England's wider empire; and thence only can come the vigour to create, whence comes the power to conceive. If England is to be an empire of the future, she must be the England of manufacturers. And the logical consequences are the reform bill and the repeal of the corn laws. But fatal as is such a struggle to the efficiency and character of national action, even in its mildest shape, there are conditions of political society in which the conflict of vast and sectional interests, concentrates into the portentous issue of a mortal strife. The confederacy of the United States has reached this period in its history. The legislation of the present Congress has effected a political revolution. It has destroyed old relations and rejected established compromises. Basing its action upon a principle recognized only by a portion of its constituency; the government, in becoming the exponent of one class, becomes necessarily also the enemy of the other. And having, in violation of traditional faith and constitutional securities, achieved its purpose, it foists an unknown language into its commentary upon the constitution, and forces upon half the commonwealth the bitter alternative of becoming subjects or rebels. The California bill and its kindred measures have been passed; the policy of the federal government firmly and distinctly declared, and the institution of slavery so far as by any possibility of constitutional construction it can be compassed, is outlawed. Under these circumstances, whether the South recognizes or rejects recent Congressional enactments, we are called on to review our position. For if we remain in the Union, we are bound by new conditions; stand in a very altered attitude, and should, at our earliest opportunity, learn to know our place. The object of these pages is, therefore, simply to ascertain what is the position of the South and what course of action it behoves us to follow in the discharge of our duties as a slaveholding people.

The vindication of slavery is no part of our purpose. We know that Providence has placed us in the midst of an institution which we cannot, as we value national existence, destroy. It has solved for us in the wisest manner, that most dangerous of social questions, the relation of labour to capital, by making that relation a moral one. It has developed the physical wealth of the country in its highest, that is, its agricultural branch, in unprecedented proportion. It has created a civilization combining in admirable measure energy and refinement. It informs all our habits of thought, lies at the basis of our political faith and of our social existence. In a word, for all that we are, we believe ourselves, under God, indebted to the institution of slavery—for a national existence, a well ordered liberty, a prosperous agriculture, an exulting commerce, a free people, and a firm government. And where God has placed us, there, without argument, are we resolved to remain, between the graves of our fathers and the homes of our children. The only questions open now for our discussion are, what are the dangers we have to meet, and what are our means of meeting them. As historical truths, affording prompt answers to these questions, we submit to the attention of every Southern man who desires to do his duty at this perilous crisis, the following propositions:

1. That all legitimate government is but the larger development of the same principles which underlie the social institutions of a nation, and that therefore the test of national health is a perfect sympathy between national government and popular institutions.

2. That the institutions of the slaveholding States are peculiar in their nature, differing in most essential features of political character from the political system of the rest of the country.

3. That this difference has excited a sectional jealousy, which, in the oplitical history of the country has deepened into sectional hostility, and that by recent legislation, the Federal Government has declared itself the ally of the North and North-west against the institutions of the South.

4. That in such a political crisis the only safety of the South is the establishment of a political centre within itself; in simpler words, the formation of an independent nation.

We shall include the two first propositions under one head, as the one is, in a great measure, but the illustration of the other.

An effort, in a practical political discussion, to resort to first principles, is always difficult, if not dangerous. For scarcely a human action, and none of the great events of history can be traced to the simple working of a single principle. And, in the varied process of investigation, terms originally clear and definite, assume necessary and sometimes strange modifications, in order to meet the exigencies of a complicated argument. The word government is a fertile illustration of these difficulties of definition. It is applied alike to the absolutism of Russia and to the republicanism of America; although this mutual application to subjects, differing not in degree, but in kind, is irreconcilable with truth. As at present used, it must mean one of two very contradictory things; either a power above and beyond the people, shaping their fortunes according to its wisdom—and it is easy to conceive such a power, deriving its origin from peculiar circumstances in national history, and thus possessed of a historical legitimacy, which a conservative philosophy would anxiously respect—or the mere administrative machinery, by which a people regulate the economical necessities of political life, and execute the resolutions of the national will. Administrations like these are widely different, and when they are loosely comprehended under the same name, it can only be, because the latter, in the exercise of necessary power, too often seeks justification in the analogies of a doubtful political generalization. It is not difficult to understand how a power like the first, independent of, and elevated above, local interest, might, with energy and wisdom, guide the course of a nation composed of very dissimilar material. Indeed, to a certain extent, the empires of Russia and Austria furnish an illustration. But where the administration is, as in the latter case, the representative of conflicting interests, the decided strength of any one great interest must, of necessity, explode the machine, or re-adjust its arrangements. It is, then, to governments of the latter character, that we more especially refer our remarks. To say of such a government, that it depends for its existence upon its conformity to popular ideas, seems almost a truism. To attempt gravely to prove that a democracy like New-York would never tolerate a House of Lords, or that a commercial people like New-England would never grant peculiar privileges to landholders, would be a waste of words and time. And the general proposition would never be questioned, were there in the country an unity of political opinion, or were the national interests divided into many classes, singly too small for preponderance, and equally scattered over the whole national territory. Unfortunately, however, the most striking feature of our physical history, is the marked development of great geographical sections; and the most important event in our industrial progress, is the creation of vast interests, bounded in their fields of action by these ineradicable geographical lines. It is true that science has achieved, over space and time, triumphs almost miraculous, but it has not annihilated them. It is true that the panting of the steam-engine and the tremor of the magnetic wire indicate an unwearied material activity, but still mountain ranges rear their heads in unbroken ruggedness—rivers roll their ceaseless currents, and oceans heave their world of waters, in discharge, now as ever, of God's great commission—to divide the nations. It is almost impossible to conquer nature. A dozen bridges across the Rhine would not identify the Frenchman and the German; a tunnel through the Alps would scarcely reconcile the Italian to the Austrian; and it is idle to suppose that the mere speed and facility of communication between distant geographical sections, will entirely counteract those national peculiarities, which it is an unerring law of Providence that those divisions shall of necessity develope.

"It was not," says a recent traveller, "until I had sailed a few miles from Lutrarki, and observed the greater clearness with which the Parnassian ranges came out, that I realized the fact, that Corinth and Delphi, two cities, morally as opposed to each other as Washington and Mecca, were yet physically so close, that the laughter of the midnight revellers might almost have met the hymns of the priests midway on the waters. What again could be more different than the character of Bœtia—sacerdotal, traditionary, unchanging—the Hellenic Austria, and that of the inventive and mercurial Attica? And yet, from the same ridge of Parnes, the shepherd descried the capitals of both. How remote from each other, in character, were Sparta—in which the whole life of man was one perpetual military discipline—and Athens, in which every one went on his own business, after his own fashion. Yet the mariner ran across, in perhaps a day's sail, from the one territory to the other, passing on his way communities unlike both."

In examining, then, the conflicting characters of two great sections, it is no unfavourable introduction to such an investigation, to discover that nature herself has drawn deeply the sectional lines. Now, if a map of the settled portion of the North American continent be prepared, indicating only the great mountain ranges and the large rivers, the most superficial review would mark three grand divisions—the north, the south, the west. The north and south this side of the Alleghanies; the west beyond it, having its Pacific border, its bold headlands looking out on Asia; its capacious harbors and its own rivers, rising, running, emptying beyond the mountains, even their sources separated by immense territories from the heights of Atlantic commerce; wealth, unbounded wealth, for its inheritance and independence, the necessary condition of its future life. Upon this side of the mountains, two great sections, divided by the Ohio and the Potomac, from the Mississippi to the Atlantic; the north possessing in the lakes and the St. Lawrence, a channel of commercial communication, reaching from Wisconsin to Maine, and the South enjoying in the Mississippi the same connection from Missouri to Florida. Not only has nature drawn these lines, but history, in the action of its providential instinct, has followed their guidance. In the colonization of this continent, who has not been struck with the marvellous parallel? The antithesis of Plymouth and Jamestown did not end with their settlement. The growth of the two great sections, radiated from different centres, diverged in distant directions, were developed from differing principles, and perfected through dissimilar experiences. For every point of likeness in the history of the two plantations, points of difference might be multiplied, and from the quaint freshness of the old chronicles might be drawn, passage after passage, expressing, in language of the most strongest symbolism, their ancient, continued, and present variance. Nor does the argument stop here. As the country has filled up, internal improvements have spread through the land, in obedience to laws hardly perhaps recognized by those who planned, and have developed, in process of completion, well defined sectional systems.

With these preparations for great national differences, no philosophical inquirer would be surprised to discover a wide distinction of sentiment and institution; and the student of political principles would anticipate the impossibility of the consistent action of a single government. What are the facts?

There is one relation, lying at the basis of all social and political life, the shifting character of which fairly indicates the national progress in wealth and civilization—the relation of labour to capital. In the history of the world, this relation has, so far, always taken one of three shapes—serfdom, slavery, or service that is voluntary labour for wages. In the two first, the relation is a moral one, or labour is a duty; in the latter, the relation is a legal one, or labour is the execution of a contract. But which ever of these shapes it has taken, the history of all that is great in achievement—all that is glorious in art—all that is wise in law, proves that the best interests of humanity require, first, that labour should be subordinate to, and controled by capital; and second, that the interests of the two should by that very dependence be as closely as possible identified. It may safely be asserted, that wherever the relation has been one of contract, the first condition only has been obtained, and that the interests of labour and capital can never be permanently or properly reconciled, except under the institution of slavery; for it stands to reason, that wherever the political theory of government recognizes the equality of labour and capital, while the great reality of society shews the one in hopeless and heartless dependance on the other, there will exist between the two a constant jealousy and a bitter strife, the weaker demanding its rights with impotent cursing, or enforcing them with revolutionary fierceness. Look for a moment at the condition of the operatives of England and France. In both the population is free, labour and capital are politically equal; while, in fact, capital tyrannizes with selfish power, holding labour to its terrible bond—the obligation a life of barely sustained toil—the penalty death by starvation. There is no moral relation between them, and the working classes who comprehend political theories only in practical results, rebel against the powers that be. In England, the chartist calls for equal representation, denounces the aristocratic institutions within which capital strives to entrench itself, and demands logically enough, we must say, that the nation should abandon the palpable inconsistency of free labour and a privileged class. In France, with still stricter and more unscrupulous logic, the socialist demonstrates that if labour and capital are equal in principle, they should be equal in practice, and that all property is theft. That this should be, reason suggests—that it ever has been, experience confirms. For while history teems with rebellions of free labour against royal power, and feudal prerogative and class privilege—revolutions which have overthrown dynasties and changed constitutions, we challenge a solitary example in the whole scope of the world's record, where slave labour has risen in successful protest against national authority, or even forced from privileged power a single political concession. The Hebrew commonwealth, in the progress of its Divine mission, spread into the proportion of a magnificent monarchy, and again shrunk into the insignificance of a scattered people, and the foundations of its slave institutions were unshaken. The kingdoms of Greece sprung struggling from their cradles, but in the perpetual strife which strengthened their manhood, the institution of slavery never perplexed their economy, nor escaped their control. The Roman governed the world, and his million of slaves never changed an Emperor, nor lost him a province. In the ancient world, the relation of labour and capital took the shape of slavery, and what disturbance did it work? In the modern world, it has taken the shape of service, and what civil commotion, what parliamentary perplexity has it not wrought? What political question is so terrible to English statesmen as the condition of England question? What combination more fearful for French politicians than the organization of labour? Without dwelling on this truth, which is capable of an infinity of illustration, we have arrived at the first great contradiction between the institutions of the North and the South. At the North, the relation of labour and capital is voluntary service; at the South, it is involuntary slavery. At the North, labour and capital are equal; at the South, labour is inferior to capital. At the North, labour and capital strive; the one, to get all it can; the other, to give as little as it may—they are enemies. At the South, labour is dependant on capital, and having ceased to be rivals, they have ceased to be enemies. Can a more violent contrast be imagined. The political majority of the North represents labour—the political majority of the South represents capital—can the latter suffer the power of legislation in the hands of the former? Free labour hates slave labour—capital, at the mercy of labour, is jealous of capital owning labour—where are their points of sympathy?

And it requires but ordinary sagacity to see that this difference of relation between labour and capital, necessitates for the North and South the development of two individual and inconsistant systems both of representation and taxation. If representation be adjusted according to the Northern principle of equality of labour and capital, the foundation of the social and political state of the South—the subordination of labour which is slave to capital, which is master, is at once overturned. If on the other hand, representation be based upon the Southern principle of property, the support of the Northern society, the equal right of every individual constituent of the Commonwealth, is stricken away, and in order to maintain political existence, the North would be forced to the creation of a privileged class from individuals claiming equal rights. And it may be here remarked that, wherever labour and capital have been recognised as theoretically, equal society has been forced in self-preservation, to the creation of artificial privileged classes. Equality of rights and privileges can, in the nature of things, exist only where the participants of political power form a separate class, and the labour of the country is subjected to it. Where this separation of labour and capital is adjusted between people of the same race, there will be more or less of struggle—but where the separation is drawn with the distinctness of colour, the political necessities of this antagonism, assume the character of providential arrangements, and execute themselves in harmony with the highest and purest moral feeling.

That this strife has not yet developed itself in fierce commotion, is owing to circumstances which are fast vanishing; that it must come, the whole history of Northern politics declares, and society is busy in preparing the elements generated between the two extremes. Now these two systems are irreconceivable either in their principles or their practice, reason and experience pronounce that can never be joined together.

In the Constitution of the United States, they have both been comprehended—time has changed a compromise of interests into a conflict of sections, and the submission of one, or the separation of both is the only alternative. And not only does this antagonism between the two systems of labour and capital exist in the two sections, but it is aggravated by the mode in which that labour and capital is employed. The progress of time has materially altered the great national relations which form the staple of the world's political history. Consumer and producer are now the great regulating terms of political results, and, although there never has been an age in which commercial interests have not entered as influencing elements into considerations of national policy, yet never has the civilized world been so dictatorially governed by the power of trade. Facility of transport, and the immense capabilities of manufacturing invention have not merely stimulated traffic to unparralled activity, but have knit the nations together by a chain work of universal extent, and exquisite sensitiveness—and not only so, but like the nervous system of the human body, this subtle and all pervading conductor ramify as it may, spreads from one great centre—the cotton trade. The power which controls this trade, holds to a very great extent the fortunes of the world in its hand. The London Times for September 7, 1850, speaks thus, in its leader on the Diplomatic necessities of Great Britain: "What the circumstances are which would make it requisite to have an able officer representing England, in a particular country can easily be conceived. A country may have by its position and power, a great influence upon our well being, or it may be intimately connected with us by commercial relations. Two countries in the world peculiarly represent these classes, France and the United States. France has in past times occupied the first place in our regard because we have for ages been at war with her, our nearest and most powerful neighbour on the Continent. America is of far more importance commercially. The commerce of France is of little importance, that with America transcends all others." Now where has nature placed the great controlling power of American commerce? In the South and as an unavoidable inference, does it follow that the industrial economy and the system of foreign relations of the nation, so far as based on commercial principles, should spring from, and be controlled by the cotton growing States. Why is it otherwise, but that in the nation there is another section supported by interests antagonist to these, in other words, a section which is in fact, a foreign power. We have shown that in the vital principle of political organization, the relation of labour and capital, the North and the South are irreconceivably hostile, that their social and political systems cannot co-exist—that the one in the nature of things wages internecine war against the other. Now we need not attempt to prove that cotton can be produced in quantities sufficient for the world's wants, only where labour and capital stand in the relation of master and slave. Experience has decided that question if it has settled no other. What is the result? Why that throwing aside the variance in the systems of representation and taxation above referred to—the North and South are diametrically opposed to each other on those most essential political relations which govern the wealth, the civilization, the national existence of the South. More than this—the vast extent and pre-eminent influence of the cotton trade divide the commercial nations of the world into two classes—those who produce cotton and those who manufacture it. They are, it is true, mutually dependant; but, according to that principle of selfishness which God has for wise purposes implanted in every breast, they are each bent on using the other at the lowest remuneration—each wishes to have the best of the bargain, and between foreign nations this is all right; this competition has served, and will serve wise purposes. Now to which class does the northern section of this confederacy belong? What greater sympathy does the North feel for us as a cotton growing section than is felt by England? Does a cotton bale meet any more fraternal regard in the way of prices in New-York than it does in Liverpool? What more sympathy is there between the southern planter and the abolition manufacturer of Lowell, than exists between him and the spinner of Manchester? We speak the same language with both—our historical associations cluster upon English soil with more fervour and frequency than upon the coast of Dutch Manhattan—our transactions with the Englishman count up in larger ciphers? What makes the one less a foreigner than the other, but the assumed right of our northern brother to meddle that he may mar? And we say boldly that it would be as wise, as safe, as honourable, to trust our domestic institutions and our foreign interests to the Parliament of Great Britain as to a Congress with a northern majority. Nay, wiser and safer, for her colonial experience has taught England never again to sacrifice her profits to her philanthropy.

Again. Our foreign relations are every day assuming growing and graver importance. And here the same antagonism of interest developes itself. The two principles of the foreign system of the great Northern section, as expressed by their statesmen and leading journals, being, 1. The extension of their commercial interests in foreign markets, bringing them into active diplomatic rivalry with Great Britain; and, 2. The manifestation of a spirit of propagandist licence, inspiring them to intermeddle in the domestic struggles of every foreign nation, where there arises a contest between constituted authority and revolutionary restlessness. The annexation of Canada, which is fast becoming from a remote speculation, a matter of party policy. The hasty welcome to the socialist government of France—a government which signalized its brief history by colonial emancipation and domestic bankruptcy—the demagogue denunciation of the Austrian court—are all significant indications of popular sentiment and national systems. Now look at the position of the South—cultivated by a slave population—supplying the staple of the world's manufacture, and ranged in imposing strength around the Gulf of Mexico, so as to command the trade of the Isthmus connection—what should be the foundation principles of her foreign relations. 1. A close alliance with the few great manufacturing nations, an anxiety to see them creating markets and multiplying their production; and, 2. An unchangeable resolution to leave the interior affairs of other nations to their own discussion, and a careful abstinence from all legislative reflection on foreign institutions, which, like our own, may be censured only because they are not comprehended. With these two basis of foreign action, and the command of the Gulf and the cotton trade, the South would be, in the maturity of her strength, the guardian of the world's commerce—the grave and impartial centre of that new balance of power, which, at no distant day, will be adjusted by the experience of the old and the energy of the new world, working together for the best interests of humanity.

It would be easy to illustrate, in a more special manner and in fuller detail, these sectional differences in social systems—in industrial interests—in foreign policy. But such an analysis would run too parallel with party history, which it is our anxious desire to avoid, and our conclusions upon which, we are afraid, would be acceptable to none. But, surely enough has been said to indicate the grounds upon which we may justly, and with no exaggeration, conclude that the Institutions of the two sections are diametically opposed. If it can be proved that the government is with the Northern section of the Confederacy, the utter want of sympathy between that Government and the South, is, as a consequence, established—the due relation between the two is broken, and we must look for safety at home. What, then, is the position of the Government? Our answer is very brief: The sense of wrong is too strong for the elaboration of syllogisms. There never yet was an honest feeling that did not spring from a correct thought. We feel that we are weak—it cannot take us long to think out the same conclusion. We will avoid a metaphysico political discussion on the checks of the Constitution. The experience of the last twenty years, from General Jackson downwards, has proved that the President, as has been admirably said, "is a demagogue by position"—that the House of Representatives represent popular passions and interests—that in the Senate only is to be found the conservative element of government. Now the representative majority is Northern—the Presidential electoral majority is Northern—and since the admission of California, the Senatorial majority is Northern. Can a multiplication table work out results more certain. If the government obeys the popular spirit which creates and sustains it, what must it do but reflect Northern sentiment, sustain Northern interests, impersonate Northern power. For argument sake, we will admit that the admission of California is right—that a savage greediness for gold is the purest of social bonds—that a State is admirably adapted to influence national legislation, where its heads are the shrewdest of speculators and its body the outcasts of every population under heaven. We will admit that Texas ought to pocket, in an extravagance of jockeying triumph, her ten millions, and chuckle at the market price of patriot blood and State pride—she may have more to spare, and she has found a generous customer. We will admit that Virginia and Maryland are but intruders in the District of Columbia, and if not acceptable, should be removed without even notice to quit; they gave the land to their Northern brethren—what more have they to do with it. We will admit, with Mr. Toombs, that the South has nothing at all to complain of, but as we do not know what we may have to censure, we earnestly ask every Southern man to take a list of the States and having separated the two sections, make the simplest of calculations, and then, with neither the fear nor favour of party before his eyes, answer the question, What is the position of the South? In case—and we may in argument imagine so improbable a thing—in case our rights should be attacked, where is our constitutional protection? The mournful but indignant echo from the past answers—where? If, then, the lessons of experience are worth the reading—if the political events of the last few months are not illusions—if the expression of outraged feeling all through our Southern land, be any thing but the wild ravings of wicked faction—it is time for the South to act firmly, promptly, and for ever. But one safe path is open to her honour, and that is, Sécession and the formation of an Independent Confederacy. Another plan has indeed been proposed and sanctioned by great names, but to us it seems either impracticable or identical with the first. It is a re-adjustment of the constitutional compact, so as to recognize the independence of each section as to its domestic policy. The formation of a Union somewhat analagous to the German confederation, by which a Zollverein should regulate our industrial policy and a Diet controul our foreign relations. That this can be obtained from the North without force, we do not believe, and the only circumstances under which such an arrangement could be effected, would be the absolute national independence of the two sections and their willingness to enter into treaty stipulations with each other, as to such interests as might be common between them. So far, then, this scheme implies secession. But we do not honestly think that the elements of our political constitution could be combined after such a fashion, and with this reference we leave the subject. What are the objections to the first course of action? They shall be stated as strongly as we have been able to find them—in the language too of Southern men. At a meeting of the citizens of Bibb county, in Georgia, on Sept. 28, 1850, a report was adopted, which uses the following language:

"The dangers that would attend a dissolution of the Union, we regard as palpable and imminent. In our opinion, it would be followed by the most disastrous consequences.

"1. It will gain for the South no additional guaranties for her cherished institutions. It will not check the spirit of fanaticism at the North, nor secure the extension of slavery into California.

"2. It will result in a civil, perhaps servile war, which would absorb all our resources, force us into a system of direct taxation, and render property less secure than at present, both in Georgia and in the border States.

"3. It would compel the slaveholders in the border States to push their negroes into the Southern markets, and thus force the planters of Georgia and adjoining States to *pay* Virginia, Kentucky and Maryland for manumitting their slaves.

"4. It would force the more southern States ultimately to *secede again* from the new confederacy, or to fall back upon separate organizations, and thus give to the South a set of petty States, without either power or respectability.

"5. Under such circumstances, the people of the South would have neither men nor money with which to carry slavery into California. They would not be able to retain it at home, much less to force it across to the shores of the Pacific.

"6. All these causes, operating conjointly, would limit the area of slavery to a few of the South Atlantic and Gulf States—where the lands would soon become exhausted—where slave labour would cease to remunerate—where the slaves themselves would be worthless, and the institution become a *tax* upon the people.

"7. The final result of the whole matter would be, that the owners would be compelled to *abolish slavery* in self-defence—because the property itself will become valueless, and they would have no means left to support it!

"Here, then, are some of the curses of dissolution; and, in our candid opinion, if the Union is severed, it will not require a quarter of a century to consummate this grand scheme of mischief and ruin."

Our analysis of these objections will divide them into two classes: 1. That a secession of the Southern States cannot be effected without war, civil or servile—perhaps both. 2. That, if effected, it would not answer the purposes of its formation.

The first objection is not a legitimate one. It is simply a selfish unwillingness to suffer, in order to succeed. If the rights in question are worth a struggle, the necessity of the conflict is no argument against the propriety of action. If the duty of the citizen is clear, the perils of the strife become patriotic privileges, and the fact that war is inevitable only proves to what an extent we have endured before we have ventured to resist—only demonstrates the power of that unrighteous authority against which we are forced to arm. We say nothing in mitigation of the unimaginable horrors of a civil war—dangers are not disarmed by self-deception, and if these terrors lie direct in our path, look at them full but firmly; but there are more terrible disasters than war, and in the perpetual cry of peace, peace, there is as much selfishness as sense. This world is not one of peace—its wisest and highest teacher brought into its troubled life "not peace but a sword," and nothing of national greatness or individual good has been achieved without sacrifice and sorrow. It is a truth of history, untouched by an exception, that no nation has ever yet matured its political growth without the stern and scarring experience of civil war. The God of this world's history is indeed the God of Hosts, and he who shrinks, in the plain path of duty, from that last appeal to arms, is not more holy than he is wise. But, while prepared for any consequence, where is the probability of civil war resulting from Southern secession? In the first place, what motive would influence the North to an invasive war? If there be any truth in the protests of our Northern brethren—if slavery be a burden to their consciences, why interfere against an Exodus which would carry with it the plague—why not let the South and slavery go together? It can only be because the industrial prosperity of the North is, to a great degree, dependent upon Southern labour and Southern consumption. If this be so—and every financial document proves it—if this be so, the question submitted to Northern statesmen may be stated thus: As a nation, we draw our wealth, in great measure, from the Southern production of cotton and the Southern consumption of our manufactured cotton. Federal legislation enabled us to benefit by that production and to control the remuneration on that consumption. The South has seceded, our relations are broken; in what way can they be restored? Shall we fight? To do so we must make up our minds to stop our manufactories; to give up our supply of cotton; to surrender our Southern market, for a time at least, to English rivals—bear up against the financial embarrassments necessary on such a state of things, and undertake, at the same time, the maintenance of a costly army and navy, and the support of a distant war: for we must act offensively. Will this pay, if it succeeds, and is success certain? The present army and navy would, to a large extent, be unofficered, the whole body of Southern officers having resigned—among them experienced, efficient, able men, fitted to organize Southern forces. Then the war of the revolution and the war of 1812 have proved that Southern armies subsist themselves on their own soil, with half the trouble and expense that foreign forces must employ. The military experience of the country points to the South as emphatically the region of soldiers; and, lastly, can such a war be protracted for a period sufficient to affect Southern prosperity or Southern spirit, without the interference of those great foreign powers whose commerce is controlled by the cotton manufacture, and who would be most materially injured by a suspension of American trade? Who can, for a moment, doubt the conclusion at which Northern sagacity would arrive? If the South acts unitedly, the apprehension of civil war is the idlest of fears. As to a servile war, we have scarcely patience to refer to it. We do not believe that any man, born and bred at the South, reared among negroes and familiar with their habits, ever entertained such an idea. We have passed through two wars, and we have yet to read the record of one servile insurrection of any military consequence, and may in all justice decline reply to an argument which cannot base itself on even a respectable probability.

So much for the first class of objections. Now let us look at the second, viz: that Southern secession, if successful, would not effect its purposes. And the first point to be settled is, what are those purposes? why should we secede? We honestly believe that much of the unwillingness that does undoubtedly exist in some quarters, to concerted Southern action, springs from a misconception on this point. Many think that we are called upon to rebel against practical oppression—to overturn some special congressional enactment—and we are in consequence met by such replies as, "How am I oppressed?—you cannot un-State California. If Texas chooses to sell her lands how can we complain?

The true position of the South is this:—From the formation of the government there have existed, in the two great sections of the Union, political systems, opposed in principle. Recent events have developed into excited hostility these contradictions, and, just at the time when sectional interests are most antagonistic, the government, by the admission of Calfornia, has destroyed the balance of power between the two sections, and placed the South, its interests, and its institutions, in helpless dependence upon Northern majorities. Will not the establishment of a Southern confederacy, with a homogeneous population, and an united government, relieve the South from this false and dangerous situation, enable her to control her own fortunes, and use, to the best advantage, the strength of her natural position.

The prime element of national Southern strength, is commerce; the peculiar character of the Southern staple identifying agriculture and commerce more completely than in any other national experience. It is in relation to commericial questions, that the South would come in contact with foreign powers, and by her industrial policy, that she would influence remote countries. Rivalry, on these points, with foreign nations, exists only in the northern section of the republic. The formation of an independent Southern confederacy, would give to the South the control of its industrial policy and its commercial connection; thus arming it, at the very outset of its national career, with diplomatic power, and at the same time, from the character of those interests, propitiating all foreign jealousy, and inviting the cordial alliance of European powers. The advantages of such a position are incalculable, and the most selfish interests of the foreign world would be prompted to a speedy recognition of our national independence. When we consider too, that completion of the Isthmus connection promises to make the Gulf of Mexico the theatre of a mightier commerce than that which, in the days of ancient Rome, civilized the classic shores of the Mediterranean, and gave the provincial city of Alexandria a place among the capitals of history, or that which illuminated with its treasure the pages of Venetian and Genoan story, we must acknowledge that the formation of a Southern confederacy, at least so far as regards its foreign relations, bids fair to place the South, an equal among the nations of the earth.

If then secession fails in its purpose, it can only be in respect to its domestic policy. What do we expect in this regard? That a homogeneous people, governed by the same sentiment and acting upon the same interests, will give to their government unity of character, and thus that parties will be formed by a fair difference of opinion on national measures, and not upon theoretical differences as to the nature of the government itself. That the government placed in immediate and active sympathy with popular institutions, will devote itself to the practical perfection of those institutions, and will cut off all extraneous agitation. Of course we can no more prevent the expression of Northern sentiment at the North, than we can check the eloquence of Exeter Hall in London, but then the agitation at the North will affect us only in the same degree. As to the expression of opinion, the world may think as it pleases, and say what it thinks. We do not complain of Northern sentiment, except where having achieved political representation, it undertakes to act in Congress. Through the national councils only does it reach us, and there only do we protest against it. England and Massachusetts—Lord Palmerston and Gov. Briggs—both think the law of South-Carolina, imprisoning colored seamen, a very unfeeling measure. They are both opposed to it in sentiment. But when the practical action of that State brought the question before the British Parliament, Lord Palmerston very wisely said that nothing could be done, foreign powers made their own police law. When the same question came before the Massachusetts Legislature, Gov. Briggs appealed to the constitution, and sent an ambassador to dispute our rights on our own soil. To this extent, then, at least, an independent government could and would check agitation; would suppress that of which only we complain, *legislative agitation.* But, says the report above quoted, all this may be true as to the body of the confederacy, but you must sacrifice the border States; and of course as this abandonment of the border States will only make new States on the narrowed border, there will follow another series of sacrifices, and the great Southern confederacy will be thus border on to destruction. This may be witty, it is scarcely wise. We have been so long accustomed to have the ocean on one side, and a blank wildness on the other, that the sense of neighbourhood with certain politicians, is a fearful experience. They cannot realize that two nations can be at peace in each other's presence. With them, 'tis distance that gives safety to the view. Now, in the first place, as agitation would be expected on these borders, it would be guarded against, and if the price of liberty is eternal vigilance, we would not complain of paying the same price for slavery.

But, in the next place, agitation would be very cautious how it crossed the line, when on the other side it had no common constitution to appeal to, and realized the risk of trial by the laws of the offending party. Even fanaticism is not reckless of its own safety. Again, there are two sides to this same border difficulty. If Virginia and Maryland and Kentucky are border States, so are Ohio and Pennsylvania. Now, if the argument be that these first States will be more exposed to the spoliation of their property, Ohio and Pennsylvania will be more exposed to the evils of retaliation. It is not to be supposed that a Southern government would fold its arms quietly at such a violation of its territory, and is it any more supposable that Ohio and Pennsylvania would allow their borders to be infested by a set of miscreants, whose action would be to draw on these States the evils of a perpetual border warfare. Indeed, if selfishness has not lost its cunning, the border States of a Northern confederacy would be the safest neighbours for their border brethren of the South. The arguments of the report as to the deterioration of the value of slaves, is of course based upon the successful result of this agitation. If, therefore, there be any justice in our argument, that not only will the South have the power, but that it will be the direct interest of the Northern border States, to suppress agitation, the whole force of the report on this head is broken. The weakness of this position could be demonstrated from other points of view, but they would not come within the scope of the present argument. Enough of the report and its resolutions.

One more objection, and we have done. There are many men who have grown old in the Union, who feel an honest and pardonable regret at the thought of its dissolution. The enthusiasm of their boyhood, the hopes of their manhood, the calm honours of their age belong to the completed circle of the past. They have felt themselves parties to the great experiment of political self-government, they have prided themselves on the successful demonstration of that great problem, and they feel that the dissolution of the Union, proclaims a mortifying failure. But it is not so. The vital principle of political liberty is representative government, and when federal arrangements are discarded, that lives in original vigor—it has become the characteristic of our race, to spread with our emigrant millions over continents, and into the hidden isles of distant seas. Who does not consider the greatest triumph of the British constitution, the facility with which it adapted itself to the altered condition of its colonies—the vigour with which under slight modifications, it developed into the great republican government, under which we have accomplished our national progress.

And so it will be with our own constitution; the elements of constitutional liberty, may be slightly varied in their action under different governments; but they will act with energy for they have been incorporated into the national character. The experiment instituted by our fathers will receive its highest illustration and a continent of great republics, equal, independent, and allied, will demonstrate to the world the capabilities of republican, constitutional government. That the dissolution of the Union must come, even without the present agitation, at no distant day, is almost a historical necessity; for the history of the world is the record of the aggregation and dissolution of great [illegible]. National individuality seems to be the agent of Providence in the conduct of the world, and having, in the extension of our territories to the extremest Western verge accomplished the first part of our destiny, we are about to fulfil the second in creating those separate national interests and individual national peculiarities, to the attrition of which is due the varied and brilliant civilization of modern times.

We have thus endeavoured to suggest the elements of the present discussion. The question is the gravest that can well be imagined—it is invested with a solemn responsibility, and rises above the flippant passion and uncertain temper of ordinary politics. We believe that the interests of the southern country demand a separate and independent government. We believe that the time has come when such a government can be established temperately, wisely, strongly. But in effecting this separation, we would not disown our indebtedness, our gratitude to the past. The Union has redeemed a continent to the christian world—it has fertilized a wilderness, and converted the rude force of nature into the beneficent action of a civilized agriculture. It has enriched the world's commerce with the untold wealth of a new and growing trade. It has spread over the vast territories of this new land the laws, the language, the literature of the Anglo-Saxon race. It has developed a population with whom liberty is identical with law, and in training thirty-three States to manhood, has fitted them for the responsibility of independent national life. It has given to history sublime names, which the world will not willingly let die—heroic actions which will light the eyes of a far-coming enthusiasm. It has achieved its destiny. Let us achieve ours.

www.ingramcontent.com/pod-product-compliance
Lightning Source LLC
LaVergne TN
LVHW020636110826
845149LV00004B/1227